About the Author

Born and raised on the coast of Rhode Island, Briana Elizabeth Turnbull is a poet and artist. Her writing covers themes such as trauma, growth, grief, and self-love. Her admiration for the craft of writing began at a young age and has been used as a method for healing throughout her lifetime. As a first-time author, she resides in New York.

Heal

Briana Elizabeth

Heal

Olympia Publishers
London

www.olympiapublishers.com
OLYMPIA PAPERBACK EDITION

A CIP catalogue record for this title is
available from the British Library.

ISBN: 978-1-80074-823-1

This is a work of fiction.
Names, characters, places and incidents originate from the writer's
imagination. Any resemblance to actual persons, living or dead, is
purely coincidental.

First Published in 2023

Olympia Publishers
Tallis House
2 Tallis Street
London
EC4Y 0AB

Printed in Great Britain

Dedication

To the healers and the humble.

Chapters

Prologue

Cold rapid hands
draw back one by one
the bandages of dark
I open my eyes
still
I am living
at the center
of a wound still fresh
-   Octavio Paz

A light went off inside me the first time I heard the phrase 'vicarious trauma.' A new connection was drawn between the sustained circle of memories that lived in my mind and the years that I had spent trying to dismiss them. Could I feel the heartache others shared and see it as my own? Was their pain mine to carry? My body would often fill with fear in these moments of uncertainty. In the way that a glass of water fills to its brim, I hoped that with time, my mind and body would heal from the wounds that I carried and become full again.

In two and a half decades, I have taken, given, and endured. Working day in and day out to understand the world that I live in while moving towards making peace with a childhood that often left me at the center of my own sorrow. In the same ways that love has known love, I now know that pain has known pain.

From my thoughts and my words to my friendships and my family – they have all come full circle with time. We understand and learn more together than I've ever taken the time to realize. For that, I feel gratitude.

In these words, you will find guilt, shame, anger, joy, relief, kindness, and love. For a moment, you may even understand my journey and what has brought me to this point.

But while you are reading, I hope you take the time to breathe. If you feel a tear roll down your cheek, I hope you remember that you are loved. If you have carried the same pain, I hope you remember the strength you hold in the present. And if you smile, I hope you know that joy is waiting for you in every corner of this life.

These moments are what matter. More than I can convey in words.

Chapter 1

Sorrow

Like water from a well, we were resources.
We weren't children; we were forces.
At the crossroads of your life.
Where ospreys nest and monarchs rest.
Your iniquity brought us to this day
and yet there was no other way.
Your temper lives within your bones.
Covered by a pain so deep.
How many more generations must grow weak?
– family

Young yet wise.
Do you remember the grief?
No more family.
No more me.
I had no choice.
I had no say.
Split time was to be the way.
I grieved my home.
I lost my bed.
The pine trees and flowers
would soon be dead.
I had no words.
I was too young.
A nimble mind
that would soon be numb.
Hate grew in me every day.
Here I write her down to lay.

Kicking rocks into the sea.
Embers that once glowed.
I lost the kid in me.
Sadness met with silence.
The ice of winters stroll.
Soft young skin with eyes of gold.
Divorce still took its toll.

Braided together.
Bonded by silk.
The coward in me,
learned how to be.
Wet feet, oxygen-free.
Irises grow
in tomorrow's weeds.
Beholden to a past
no longer for me.
Codependence
felt like it
may never flee.

Salt in my wounds.
Weight on my shoulders.
Reminded that in my loneliest moments,
I wasn't in love with the company that I held.

A soul in concrete.
Weathered hands grasp metal bars.
A heart that still beats.
Stale air, stale clothes.
Pen to paper
on trees that are sold.
Societies fool.
Mounded like dirt.
Reform they will preach.
Learn how to be.
Left only with time.
A dream to be free.
The seasons will change.
In spring,
Dahlias grow new.
In the garden
under weeping willows,
we wait for you.

In fields without doves.
In stories without soul.
In storms without sun.
In a love that tries to run.
Worry lives.

I am you.
You are me.
We are stories
that mirror the soul.
Fragments of
a life untold.

A home through time:
Moss covered treehouse.
Miles of woods.
A roof so roaring.
Ten first drawings.
Sister's old bookshelf.
One less parent.
Grass that's dying.
Ice cold morning.
Family that's broken.

In the land that God forgot.
Where a man gets blue.
In the middle of nowhere.
Twelve thousand miles from you.
A nation taught to take.
Overseas you grew.
Demoralized daily.
Home awaited.
Anger understated.
No ambiguity in the epitaph of a veteran.
Paralyzed by parallels.
War made a man out of you.
War took a home from you.
Paralyzed by parallels.
Home made a soldier of you.
Home took safety from you.

A voice engulfed in hate is hard to deny.
I felt my stomach clench and knew that it would
be years until I would feel it release again.

Did you remember to feel the air on your face?
Or did you only feel it with tears,
while you held on through the years?

They call you a tornado.
Your anger tears down worlds.
They call me a tsunami.
My sadness sweeps in as waves.

You sit with your lies.
It is there that you learned to rely.
Rather than grow, you live your life through lows.
You see others' pain, but yours must come first.
For without your vice, you're only a curse.

You taught us how to react.
We taught ourselves how to listen.
– action, reaction

I have not yet known you in my heart.
I have seen you from afar. I fear your power.
– loss

I've ignored you for as long as I can remember.
I feel you when my family doesn't see me
and doesn't wish to stay close to me.
In jealousy comes anger.
I must learn to let you go.

– resentment

Time and time again
We fell down a rabbit hole
You took from our souls
Time and time again
We learned to let go

Before it was anger, it was confusion.
An overwhelming grief that I didn't have
anyone, except for myself.
– conflict

The hate you felt embodied in us as we grew.
From the root of a tree, you watered us with oil.

I cried
For days and months and years
Until one day, I felt so empty
My stomach so dry
There was nothing left to cry

Fire to my woes.
Molten iron to the soul.

Candles that forget
to light the way.

Lit by matches
waiting to decay.

Old patterns
sewn into the seams of our life.

Waiting for ice cold mornings.
December's freeze, winter's frost.

Hearts that know of hot and cold.
When do we bury these highs and lows?

In my heart you lived.
False compassion stemmed from guilt.
Scrutinized by secrets.
Your words lived within each of us.

The weight felt as if we'd tumbled under waves.
In the dark, we learned to live as we held onto each breath.
When we took the time to feel the knots wrapped in our
stomachs, we learned to let them go. Forgiveness took us decades,
but in it, we found our peace.

Mind and body. Body and mind.
You reminded me every day you were one.
– neglect

Different times.
They blamed their ignorance.
It made no difference.
You blurred the lines
of our innocence.

To live in this body
means to guide from
a place unknown.
Still young
in the stories that
I tell myself.
Does vanity own me?
Or is vanity dressed as a man
defining what beauty means
through preconceived notions
and magazines.
The image I see
is still through your eyes.
Slowly, I break free
and see me for me.
With beauty far deeper
than the eye can see.
In words that make meaning
and work that takes time.
In more than vanity
that costs just a nickel or dime.

Mistaken mentors.
Soul-starved by manipulation.
A culture taught to take.
Demanded not to break.

Light gone.
Money strong.
Superficiality.
Lack of fulfillment.
The part of me looking for security.
Claimed by capitalism.

Diluted confidence.
Every word held consequence.

The closer I am to the clouds.
The heavier you feel.
The deepness of the ocean.
The loss of complete control.

I've come to know you in my bones.
– fear

We saw wildfires burn the west.
Our lungs were put to the test.
Fog clouded every inch of the horizon.
We felt miles of commotion.

You showed us what happened when we didn't care
for what we loved most.
– mother earth

Connected, intertwined like vines.
You held more power than currents.

Shames power sits with me at dawn.
Conditioned to live with the guilt we carry.

There are days when I forget to feel.
The motions replace waves.
– time you can't get back

You see me, I see myself.
You hold me, I feel myself.
You love me, I love myself.
– disillusioned

Spiderwebs line
every wall of the space
we held close.
I told myself a story.
One as old as time.
Where the wind
fell through old bamboo.
You told me that whiskey
was an acquired taste
as if I didn't know.
Booze, booze, booze.
You had no better friend.
Alcohol showed up for you
more than any person ever could.
All the things we never did.
You were on your own trip.
The story I remember.
The story stained
on the bottom of my converse
that I've had since I was 10.
Bottom of the bottle,
just another man's best friend.

You are my highs and my lows.
You manifest my best decisions and my worst.
You've crossed oceans with me and buried
yourself in shame with me.
I avoid you; I love you.
– impulse

You asked me to love the parts of myself
that were hard to remember still lived.

I sit surrounded by fragile men.
Where egos shatter like glass.
May women raise boys with empathy.
To be men with less expectation
and more celebration.

A letter to my sister.
The weather lacks warmth
but I found a home in New York again.
Two thousand dollars and four walls later.
I'm back to where we started.
Isn't it crazy that if our childhood didn't happen
exactly the way it did, I might not be here.
But then again, maybe I would be.
Roll the dice.
Make a bet.
I could make it.
Truth is the city never sleeps.
They weren't lying.
My eyes have learned to live with this kind of tired.
Protests still line corners of the streets
with signs that tell of troubling times.
Is it 2023 or 1933?
I thought progress came in parallel.
But now I'm not so sure.
The leaves are dying.
The birds are flying.
Men are rich.
Men are poor.
What's left in this city that we still adore?

In the woods,
smokestacks linger.
You're wrapped in cotton.
One leg in the sheets,
the other kicking me.

I can feel the winter on your lips.
Words that burn, language that lingers.
Every time I needed you, it came at a cost.
We were lost. Every November, I still remember.
Our last fall in New York.

A Saturday in Brooklyn.
I call my grandma.

Laundry drying.
Quarters stacked.

Ask her about life without Pa.
Good days, bad days.

She whispers that the worst days are numb.
No feeling, yet tears will still flow.

I can hear my voice when she speaks.
A pain we both know.

Miles away with so much love.
Still, we learn we must let go.

Pride aside, with hearts left open.
You thought you knew, a past so blue.

We gave it an hour.
Then we gave it a day.
Six years later, we needed our weekends.
Weekends turned to weeks.
We thought we'd make it last.
The good times may remind us,
but new days come in May.

I'd wake at midnight
with words that had no home.
No place to go.

They'd spin in my mind.
Reminded that I didn't have much time.
I feared grief the way you fear first times.

Would you still be with me?
Or would you live in a network
of memories only brought back
by the smell of the ocean
and old leather seats.

I can't help but think
of how much I'll miss this life
without you near me.

Our first night
in New York.
Three a.m., we couldn't sleep.
We sat on the fire escape
and the words came easy.
I wondered if we knew what love could do.
I cried every time you left.
Sweet like September.
Still like Sunday.
Time stood with me.
Reminded that it wasn't infinite.

Learned to live without high expectations.
Through days of disappointment.
You expected the world from me
but never knew patience with me.
Maybe one day, we'll learn how to love.

Still, I wonder, a life lived through thunder.
Did you shape me or remake me?

A late Sunday in May.
Light rain and long rides.
Envy sat between us.
Air thick with the
smoke of tomorrows
new beginnings.

I never saw a journey where we settled.
I saw a home.

Chapter 2

Reckon

I interpreted you through noise.
I thought you were my
accomplishments, my career.
But you were empathy and forgiveness.
You were love.
– self-growth

Wisdom and worry.
Unconditional love and pain.
You exist as one.
– mom and dad

Two and a half decades.
Taken, given, endured.

To come from cooks
means details and delicacies.
Young hands and revelries.
With care, they craft.
Healing aches with remedies.

We grow together like flowers. Hand in hand.
You see my soul; you hold me close.
You breathe life into me when I can't for
myself. You see my heart and love it whole.
– sisters & brothers

You are more precious than I ever knew.
– time

Open your eyes,
I plea.
The root of evil,
you see.
Caste systems
that we call home.
On land made
from life and bone.
Injustice each century.
Designed to be incendiary.

You told me to sit with my younger self.
Show her what she's learned.
Stay with her for a while.
There, she listened.

Touched souls.
First homes.
Deep laughs.
Long reads.
Reminded to remember.
Love that lasts forever.
– grandma

I see the lines that circle your eyes.
Crow's feet.

The stumble in your walk.
Hips that grow weak.

A life lived before me.
I try not to weep.

The love that we carry
ever-present, runs deep.

We pray that you blossom
and leave this life whole,
but only in peace, you will find we all grow.

The dreamer in you
saw the child in me.
The world through your eyes,
a place I'd soon be.
With realism shed
and love to be spread.
Your gift was your word.
Risk played its role,
I hope you can see.
For every lost venture,
I learned how to be.

I touched my hands and felt engraved lines
that had existed for lifetimes before me.
I saw birthmarks and thought of the wounds that I carried.
– old stories

A heart that hurts can grow with light.
– trying

You have the power of wars in you.
– reflection

You taught me to look inward.
To make something more out of my pain.
– spirituality

Reflecting, restarting, loving, yelling, remembering, talking, missing, working, trying, growing, giving, sacrificing, staying, hoping, living, learning.

I buried my dependence
and with it came a light.
I learned to live in peace
and gave up every fight.

I found a place for love.
Where sadness fled.
Connected only by our words.
Masters of the verbal.

With discipline came the calm.
I craved a sense of stillness
that only I could give myself.

Collected memories like seashells.
When the waves hit the sand,
I imagined every worry washed
away until new days.

What am I without you?
– hope

Old Narragansett.
Land as far as the eye can see.
Dove-grey skies
and stone-covered steps
down to the sea.
Love was mahogany,
orange peels burning,
fires with anise.
Winter meant family
and less time for me.

Freckles say I've seen warmer days.
Scars show I've known despair.
Wrinkles speak of wisdom.
Dark circles know of sleepless nights.

A student of sorts.
Buried in words.
Somewhere between
syllables and synonyms.
– the poet

Cities taught us,
everything we knew existed within us.

We drove two-hundred-seventy-five miles
from Tucson to Las Cruces.
We felt fresh air in our lungs and the sun on our faces.
It was the first time I'd felt small.
As if pieces of the world had existed for
thousands of years before me,
and I was blessed that for a small glimpse of time,
I was able to exist upon them.
I felt three tears roll down my cheek.
I've known life.
– the American southwest

You laid in the sand.
The sting of yesterday's jellyfish.
Skin swollen red.
Eyes tired from last night's Negroni.
In the sea, you saw me.
Chock-full of fear.
Still and curious
of all that is ahead of me.
Knowing that when strength felt foreign to me,
culture could cure me.

Rock covered roads.
Elderly men draped in robes.
Our shoulders touched on a corner in Morocco.
You sold saffron while I sold stories.

I could hear it in your voice.
All the years you worked
to make this world feel like a home for me.
The aches you felt in your neck and your legs.
As if I could bring them back for you.
You were the kind of joy that Sundays brought me.
But then I remembered that I love Sundays because of you.
We named every plant in your garden
and we loved to try new wines.
Some homemade, some cheap.
Don't worry, Ma.
Life's still sweet.

We met fear with desire
in a city that never tired.

In the heat of summer, we dance under the stars,
swaying lightly over sand.

The sea's breeze meets the rhythm of song,
while the women hold on.

Black hair falls over soft skin
as they spin and set eyes on the moon.

The fire burns while the base turns
and we find friendship in a melody.

In books and by bonfires.
In the depths of the sea.

I lost track of time.
I learned how to be.

In prose and prayer.
In the height of mountains and trees.

I lost track of time.
I learned how to be.

In the freedom of dance.
Where the horizon meets dawn.

I lost track of time.
I learned how to be.

Where the cliffs hit the sea,
something stirred in me.
Mid-July made us cry,
struck by every high.

We got so high. Felt alive.
Wished we could take the present with us.
You showed me joy.

We never talked about the passion
that could be read between the lines
of every conversation.
Or the heaviness in our chests
that dissipated when we laughed.
Hours on end.
One hundred books later.
Still here waiting
until we reach our best selves.

When the dust settled
And the sea was calm
When the sun rose
And the streets were still
The storm was worth the wait
For new days without old ways

Old coffee table
stained with white wine.
Remnants of last night's smoke.
Every conversation
held a little closer.
Staring at the ceiling.
The smell of ember,
sweet like summer.
– days with you

Sun hits the lime trees.
The air smells of an ocean breeze.
In a haze, I caught your gaze.
A west coast summer, like no other.

White butterfly.
Wings like water.
You reminded me of honey.
Smooth like silk,
stuck like glue.
I found myself wrapped up in you.

Chapter 3

Heal

I watched intently
as the sun kissed you.
Knowing that healing
meant learning to forgive you.
A past that was grounded in tradition.
There was power in what you taught me.

When my heart felt light the sun would burn.
Birds sang through trees.
Locals laughed.
Ladders ran deep into the sea.
Train windows shuttered.
From olive trees to new cities.
I wanted to know why you left.
What was your dream?

You made a home for me.
A feeling I long craved.
You taught me
beauty existed in small moments.
In the way the breeze lifts the trees,
in the unspoken words of birds.
In the universal language of love.

Lemon groves lined for miles.
It took twenty-seven years of praying that you'd find your way in a world that wanted you to fail. That you'd find joy in a way that only you would know.

Espresso on my lips.
Three swings of my hips.
We finally learned to love.
Rosy red cheeks, met with a sweep.

Strength is unconditional when love is not.
Don't forget this.

You gave me decades of your time.
Decades that some never get.
You conditioned me to expect
and now all I want is to take.
But I must earn, must work.

At the center of my sorrow,
I found peace.

I was raised on the shoulders of the women
that came before me.
– caregivers

You can't give the world more
than you give yourself.
– reminders

Your laughter fed my health
more than any medicine ever could.

Feet on the ground.
Roots in the earth.
I've waited for you.
– stability

I see you in gardens.
Dirt under your fingernails.
Joy in your heart.
Peace in your mind.
Knowing that with new seasons
comes new life.
– elders

Hate turned to forgiveness.
In my heart, it arrived.
Jealousy turned to empathy.
In my soul, it thrived.

With new leaves old, and with old comes new.
In dark and light, I lay with you.
– outgrowing adaptations

Don't look at grief through blue eyes.
This one isn't for you.
It's for your Ma.
You told me to show up
the same way I always did.
Loud and full of love.
To remind you that life will always be sweet.
We spent our life with Pa, down by the sea.
Ashes couldn't take that from me.
The memories would stay.
I can still smell your Old Spice
mixed with ocean breeze.
And your pear tree
looking back at me.
Gram loved roses
and I bet you knew that first.
A veteran to the world,
but a friend that put us first.
You lived a beautiful life.
Four young kids,
with hearts of gold.
A story that you would have told.
It may take time,
but please don't fret.
One day we'll pick you up in
a Red Mustang you won't forget.

Pain flies, I told myself.
Today it stays, tomorrow it fades.

Homes stacked by brick.
The countryside lay.

Autumn's crisp morning.
A stone's throw away.

White stone and beige tones.
Persian rugs and lavender tea.

Dogs howl to the moon.
Earth's feast away from the sea.

Eyes closed; air breathed.
Magpies learn to fly free.

Surrounded by elders.
Communal wisdom.
Words that stay with me
and continue to guide me.

I feel you in my spine.
You lift my shoulders and sharpen my voice.
You know me better than I know myself.
– strength

I felt my soul again when we spoke.
You taught me how to live again.
— acceptance

It has been taken from me.
I didn't see its value.
I underestimated its power.
What is left for us without time and health?

Shh, I heard the waterfall say.
It asked for my silence
and took in my presence.
It knew it held power,
but it was gentle with my stillness.

For the first time, I felt clarity.
I looked at the matters that interfered with me gaining a deeper understanding of myself, and the world around me.
I asked them to sit with me and stay for a while.
We would learn together.

— zasho

All I can ask from the world
is that it continues to share its perspective
and to teach me what I have not yet learned.
– sustaining self

May your decisions be made with conviction.
May your heart be fuller than oceans.

The years feel like skipping stones.
Onward, upward, always forward.

Challenge comes as no surprise.
Through it, we rise.

Take the world as it is and give it more.

– caring

With solitude came calm.
– knowing self

May your love be given
with the certainty of tides.
May your heart be filled with
as much light as the sun.
May your sorrow give you the
clarity of one hundred storms.

I lived for moments of fear.
In them, I felt my most present.

The unknown does not scare me.
The routine does.
To relinquish all practice and pattern
would be to know joy.

Normal is a construct.
A box with rigid edges and no room to grow.

Remember this as the year that you learned how to take care of yourself. To prioritize, to care, to learn, to understand.

What I remember about you.
Your voice was your light
and your love was your power.
You gave us all hope
in the darkest of hours.
The value of family
you carried with pride.
Your consistency came
like the evening tide.

Can you love your mind?
Like a glass of red wine.
Can you hold your sorrow?
Like there may be no tomorrow.
Can you build a foundation
with little expectation?

The color blue:
It's the story you start but never finish.
It's the calm before the storm.
It will always be home for me.
It is never mean. It does not get jealous.
It's up and it's down, the ocean and the sky.
It's a reminder that you aren't alone.

Will you live by the sea?
Where waves come in as a sense of calm.
Will you live on a lake?
Where stillness reminds you of the heart
you hold in the present.
Will you live near bookstores?
By places that take away past burdens
and remind you that there is more to learn.
Will you create a space of chaos?
Or will you walk in the woods
until every worry withers away.
Will you pick your home with sincerity
and give it the same love that has lived within you all along?

Printed in the USA
CPSIA information can be obtained
at www.ICGtesting.com
LVHW050849111123
763265LV00121B/2141